A fashionable HISTORY of the SHOE

A FASHIONABLE HISTORY OF THE SHOE
was produced by

David West 𖠋 Children's Books
7 Princeton Court
55 Felsham Road
London SW15 1AZ

Author: Helen Reynolds
Editor: Jackie Gaff
Picture Research: Carlotta Cooper
Designer: Julie Joubinaux

First published in Great Britain in 2003 by
Heinemann Library, Halley Court, Jordan Hill,
Oxford OX2 8EJ, a division of
Harcourt Education Ltd.

OXFORD MELBOURNE AUCKLAND
JOHANNESBURG BLANTYRE GABORONE
IBADAN PORTSMOUTH (NH) USA CHICAGO

Copyright © 2003 David West Children's Books

07 06 05 04 03
10 9 8 7 6 5 4 3 2 1

ISBN 0 431 18335 X (HB)
ISBN 0 431 18343 0 (PB)

British Library Cataloguing in Publication Data

Reynolds, Helen
A fashionable history of the shoe
1. Shoes - History - Juvenile literature 2. Fashion
- History - Juvenile literature
I. Title II. The shoe
391.4'13'09

Printed and bound in China

*An explanation of difficult words can be
found in the glossary on page 31.*

A *fashionable* HISTORY of the SHOE

Heinemann
LIBRARY

Contents

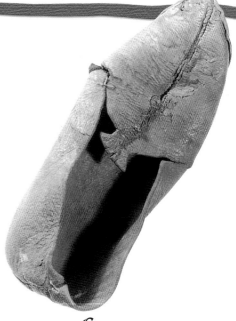

SLIPPER SHOE

This soft, leather shoe was the basic style of footwear worn by Europeans throughout the Middle Ages. It was made by sewing the upper to the sole, then turning it inside out – hence its name, the turnshoe.

SHOEMAKER'S CRAFT

Footwear was made by hand until shoemaking machines were invented in the 19th century.

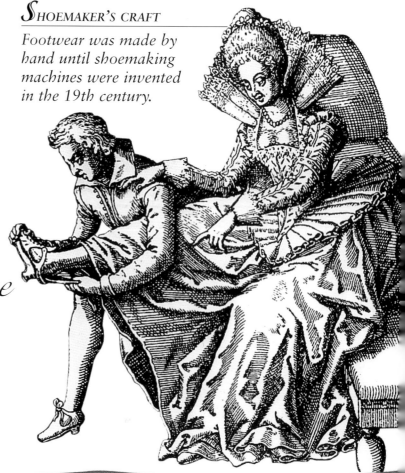

From foot bag to fashion fads

SHOES WERE INVENTED TO PROTECT FEET *from rough ground and sharp objects, as well as to keep them warm in cold weather. They date back to prehistoric times, when people made baglike foot coverings out of furry animal skins or simply wound leather strips around their feet and ankles. Over the ages, the basic design was improved until shoes had an underside called a sole and a top part called an upper. Different types of shoe were introduced, from sturdy hobnailed boots for soldiers to fragile satin slippers for court ladies. Fashions began to come and go, and just like today, some styles were sensible, others outrageously impractical.*

HIGH FASHION

Standing would be tricky in this contemporary stiletto-heeled shoe, let alone walking. Its high heel is made possible by a sturdy steel core.

CHIC SHAPE

Originally designed as sportswear, the trainer is now a fashionable everyday shoe.

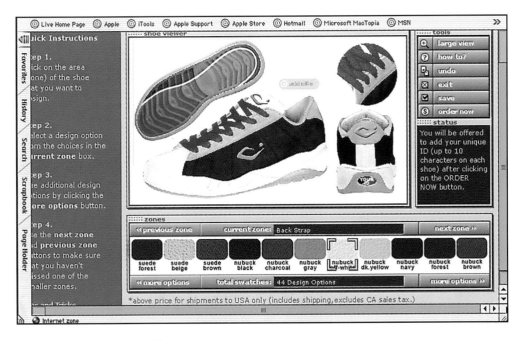

LET YOUR FINGERS DO THE WALKING

Computers are used in every stage of shoe production these days, from design to manufacture and even online shopping.

Material matters

AROUND THE WORLD, *early civilizations made shoes from the materials available to them, suiting styles to their local landscape and climate. The earliest-known ancient Egyptian shoes, for example, were woven from papyrus reeds. These simple sandals let cool air circulate around the feet while protecting them from hot desert sands.*

Looking at leather

Northern Europe's cold weather and rough ground meant that people needed more hard-wearing materials such as leather. The process of turning animal skins into leather is called tanning, and it's been practised for more than 3,000 years. The thickest leathers were made by tanning cattle hides, while softer leathers were made from the skins of deer, goats, pigs and sheep, or by splitting thick hides into thin layers.

FIRST FOOTWEAR

These Native American shoes are among the oldest yet found. This shoe, left, was woven from plant fibres 9,000 years ago. The one above was made from leather and lined with grass around 1,000 years ago.

CLEVER CLOGS

The clog is a shoe carved from a single piece of wood. An extremely hard-wearing material, wood has been used in shoemaking for thousands of years.

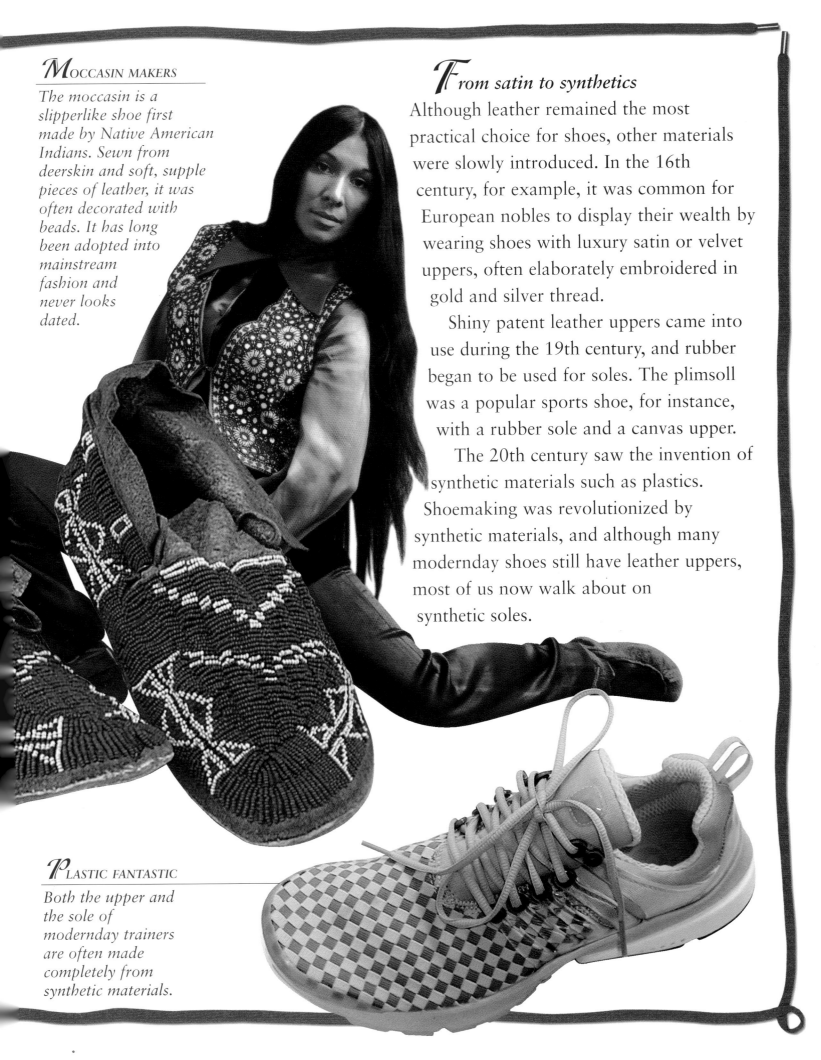

MOCCASIN MAKERS

The moccasin is a slipperlike shoe first made by Native American Indians. Sewn from deerskin and soft, supple pieces of leather, it was often decorated with beads. It has long been adopted into mainstream fashion and never looks dated.

From satin to synthetics

Although leather remained the most practical choice for shoes, other materials were slowly introduced. In the 16th century, for example, it was common for European nobles to display their wealth by wearing shoes with luxury satin or velvet uppers, often elaborately embroidered in gold and silver thread.

Shiny patent leather uppers came into use during the 19th century, and rubber began to be used for soles. The plimsoll was a popular sports shoe, for instance, with a rubber sole and a canvas upper.

The 20th century saw the invention of synthetic materials such as plastics. Shoemaking was revolutionized by synthetic materials, and although many modernday shoes still have leather uppers, most of us now walk about on synthetic soles.

PLASTIC FANTASTIC

Both the upper and the sole of modernday trainers are often made completely from synthetic materials.

Shape shifting

JUST AS FASHIONABLE DRESS HAS NOT ALWAYS FOLLOWED *the natural contours of the human body, so shoes have not always followed the shape of the foot. Changing styles have taken shoes from long and narrow to wide and wedgy and back again, with pointed, round or squared-off toes.*

Making a point

Pointed toes became the height of fashion for the turnshoe worn throughout medieval Europe. There were style victims then as today, and by 600 years ago, some noblemen were stepping out in such long, narrow shoes that they had to tie the tips to garters around their knees.

Toeing the line

Early shoes were moulded around the natural shape of the foot, but by the 12th century European shoemakers were beginning to give shoes a pointed toe. Nobles had the money to play with fashion, and by the end of the 14th century they were wearing narrow shoes with pointed tips that turned upwards. At the English court, noblemen took this fashion to such extremes they found it hard to walk, and laws were introduced to regulate shoe lengths!

During the 16th century shoes became shorter and rounder, and a style called the duckbill came into fashion. Styles began to change more frequently, and different shoe shapes went in and out of fashion.

Royal rig-out

Henry VIII of England was depicted wearing the latest fashion in this 1536 portrait, including duckbill shoes with cut-out patterns in the uppers. Padding was needed to maintain the shoes' wide shape.

TOE TORTURE

The women's pointed shoes of the sixties, unlike the soft medieval turnshoes, were stiff and unbending, and often gave their wearers corns, blisters or even bunions. Strangely, they have rarely been out of fashion!

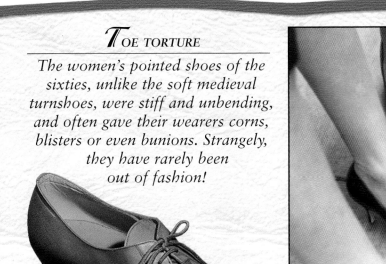

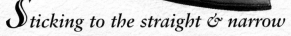

Sticking to the straight & narrow

Shoemakers were also producing footwear with absolutely straight sides by the 16th century. Instead of a pair made up of one shoe for the left foot and another for the right, both shoes were identical and could be worn on either foot. It wasn't until the middle of the 19th century that shoes were made for left and right feet.

Shoemaking machines were invented at about this time, making production quicker and cheaper. In turn, this meant that more and more people could afford to keep up with changing footwear fashions.

SQUARE ENDS

Fashions change so rapidly these days that square toes can be in one season and out the next, as rounded or pointed toes take over again.

BOUND FEET

Tiny shoes like these were once worn by women at the Chinese Imperial Court. As girls, their feet were bandaged to keep them as small as 8 cm. The practice of foot-binding was banned in 1911.

Roman remains

The soles of Roman boots and work shoes were protected from hard surfaces by metal hobnails. The hobnail had a broad head and a short spike.

Sole survivors

WHEN THE ROMANS EXPANDED THEIR EMPIRE and built paved roads throughout Europe, they needed sturdy boots for their marching soldiers. Short nails called hobnails were the answer. Hammered into the leather sole, they protected it from wear and tear.

Old boots

In medieval times, even boots were made from soft leather using the turnshoe method. Laces were leather as well.

Soft-soled turnshoes

After the fall of their empire in CE 406, the Romans' shoemaking skills were forgotten. Hobnailed boots were replaced by the slipperlike turnshoe, made by sewing an upper and a sole together and then turning them inside out. Turnshoes didn't wear well because even their soles had to be made from soft leather, so that the finished shoes could be turned inside out.

Suede & crepe

The Teddy boy styles of the 1950s included suede shoes with thick flat soles of crepe rubber. They were usually teamed with flourescent coloured socks.

Hardwearing welted shoes

Towards the end of the Middle Ages, the turnshoe began to be replaced by the welted shoe – the form of shoe construction still used today. In a welted shoe, the upper is attached to the insole, then a strip called the welt is placed between the insole and the sole. Finally, the insole, welt and sole are stitched together. Because welted shoes didn't need to be turned inside out, their soles could be made from much sturdier leather than that used for turnshoes.

These boots were made for walking

To help stop the wearer slipping, modern walking boots have synthetic soles with heavily grooved treads.

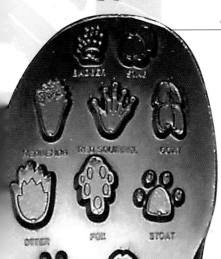

Wartime make-do

Shortages of leather during World War II (1939–45) meant that shoe soles were sometimes made of cork or wood. The wedge shape made the soles stronger.

Modern manufacturing

Sole manufacture changed very little until the 19th century. The big breakthrough came in 1858, when an American called Lyman R. Blake invented a machine for sewing the soles of shoes to the upper. Although rubber-soled sports shoes became popular in the 19th century, leather soles continued to be the first choice for other shoes until synthetic materials took over in the 20th century. Today, the majority of shoe soles are made from synthetic materials which are shaped and fixed to the upper when molten.

Animal footprints

Unlike leather soles, synthetic ones can be moulded into various shapes, including patterned treads.

Walking on air

Soles cushion our feet, as well as protecting them. Contemporary designs include trainers with air-filled soles.

Walking tall

THICK-SOLED PLATFORM SHOES WERE INVENTED *hundreds of years ago to raise the wearer's feet well above the mud and puddles of ancient streets. However, people have long had far more fashion-conscious reasons for wearing them. Platform soles make the wearer look taller and help them stand out in a crowd. In the past this also showed that the wearer was a person of great wealth and high social standing.*

Shiny chopines

The chopines worn by 16th-century Venetian ladies often had shaped platforms, which were covered in embroidered velvet and jewels.

Platformed protectors

Early platforms were sometimes slipped on as overshoes, so that more precious shoes were lifted above muddy streets.

High society

No one made more of this height advantage than the court ladies of 16th-century Venice. Venetian platform shoes were known as chopines and they could be as high as 50 cm – the wearer could only stay upright with a servant holding on to each arm to support her. This impractical style didn't really catch on elsewhere in Europe, and it was soon replaced by a new enthusiasm for high heels.

Platform shoes didn't come back into fashion until the 20th century, when advances in shoe technology resulted in more practical designs.

Natural materials

Since their invention, the soles of platform shoes have been made from wood or, like this 1970s shoe, from cork.

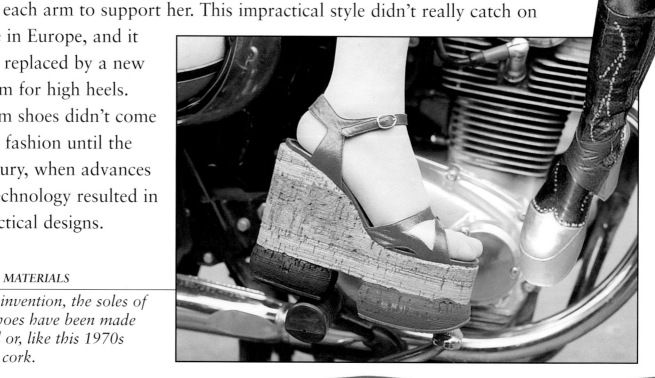

Musical madness

Teeteringly high platform soles put the finishing touch to the outrageous stage costumes worn by the Glam rockers of the 1970s.

See-through stompers

Wacky 1970s designs included platform shoes with transparent heels.

Stepping out in style

Shoe designers such as Italian Salvatore Ferragamo (1898–1960) came up with a range of innovative styles in the 1930s, including wedged platform shoes which were widely copied. Platforms remained in fashion until 1947, when the New Look brought more elegant heels back into vogue.

The remainder of the century saw two further revivals, the first championed by the Glam rock stars of the 1970s. The second came in the 1990s, when the ultra-high designs included the 20-cm platform shoe that famously tripped model Naomi Campbell during a 1994 catwalk show.

Dedicated followers of fashion

Platform shoes and boots were seen on the streets as well as on the stage in the 1970s. As in 16th-century Venice, wearers sometimes needed a shoulder to lean on to help them stay upright.

Coming to heel

NO ONE KNOWS EXACTLY WHEN OR WHY *the heel was invented. Although footwear that was raised above the ground was worn in ancient times, the shoes were probably a form of platform. Early platform shoes were notoriously difficult to get around on, and at some stage someone found that by making the heel higher than the sole you obtained height while still being able to walk about.*

Tall story?

One theory about the heel is that it was invented after the stirrup, to stop the rider's foot slipping out.

Fashionable French queen

We do know, however, that heeled shoes were worn at the French court during the 16th century. The French queen, Catherine de' Medici (1519–89), made the style popular after buying heeled shoes from an Italian shoemaker. During the next hundred years the fashion spread through the courts of Europe, with heels growing higher and being worn by noblemen and women alike.

Courting complements

These 17th-century silk shoes are embroidered with silver thread. The splayed heel is known as a Louis heel.

High-heeled shoes are completely unsuitable for farmwork and other manual labour, and for centuries they were only worn by the nobility. Made of richly decorated leather, satin or velvet, the shoes were also extremely costly. It wasn't until the 18th century that a heeled shoe was widely worn by the monied middle classes. Even then, they had lower heels than those worn by court nobles.

Victorian high fashion

High-heeled shoes were a must for fashionable ladies in the late 19th century, and replaced the flat shoes worn since the early 1800s.

In the 1920s, skirts rose to knee length and women's shoes became very visible. The shaped heels and beautiful decoration of these evening shoes are typical of the period.

Reaching new heights

Taller, more narrow heels became possible after the stiletto was invented in Italy in the early 1950s. Its strength lay in its narrow steel core, and two shoe designers are famous for developing its potential – Salvatore Ferragamo and Frenchman Roger Vivier (1913–98).

Vivier worked with the French fashion designer Christian Dior (1905–57) creating shoes to go with his postwar collections. Ferragamo was shoemaker to many Hollywood stars, including Marilyn Monroe (1926–62), and his stilettos are thought to be responsible for her famously sexy walk.

BEATLE BOOTS FANS— ARE HERE!

BLACK SMOOTH LEATHER UPPERS. ELASTIC SIDE GUSSETS.

per pr. 75/11

CUBAN HEEL

and PACKING INCLUDED
MADE ON T... ...ENT ONLY FOR:—
...LTD.
...don, N...
...OM THE
...H WITH OR...

PERENNIAL FAVOURITE

Stiletto heels are ever-popular, despite early doctors' warnings that they could result in injury. The lower-heeled version is a safer option.

WELL-HEELED CLIENTS

Cuban-heeled boots for men took off in the 1960s after Roger Vivier made them for the Beatles. Vivier's other clients included Queen Elizabeth II, for whom he designed the shoes she wore at her 1953 coronation.

The ties that bind

ALL SORTS OF SHOE FASTENINGS *have been invented over the years. The early Egyptians used a thong-style strap between the toes, while in India people gripped a knob on the shoe sole with their big and second toes. Roman shoes were tied on with leather laces, as were North American moccasins and the turnshoes of medieval Europe.*

Romance with the rose

The welted shoe had a far sturdier construction than the turnshoe, and its introduction at the end of the Middle Ages opened up more creative possibilities for ensuring that shoes stayed on the feet. Large, fabric rosettes were a popular shoe decoration at European courts during the first part of the 17th century. Often they were embroidered with gold or silver thread and small jewels to make them sparkle.

Ankle boot

Dating from the late 14th century, this child's turnshoe has leather laces to hold it safely around the ankle. The laces are threaded through holes punched into the soft shoe leather.

Ribbons and bows

By the end of the 17th century it had become fashionable for court nobles to tie their shoes with extravagant bows made from broad ribbons. Ordinary people used narrower ribbons and made smaller bows.

One, two, buckle my shoe

Metal buckles came into common use during the 18th century, while in the 19th century tightly laced or buttoned boots were popular. Elastic-sided boots date back to the 1830s. Easier to pull on or off than buttoned or laced footwear, they had been widely adopted by the early 1900s. Buttons and laces didn't vanish, though – they went in and out of fashion throughout the 20th century.

Beautiful buckles

Big, plain shoe buckles like these were all the rage at the end of the 18th century. At other times, the fashion was for highly decorative buckles.

All zipped up

The forerunner of the modern zip was the slide fastener patented by Whitcomb L. Judson in 1893 in the United States. The word 'zipper' comes from the trade name for the rubber boots with slide fasteners that were first sold by the B.F. Goodrich Company in 1923. Zips were slow to catch on, as they were not widely available outside the United States until after World War II.

Natty spats

Spats, originally of the 1890s–1900s, were cloth shoe-coverings attached by a loop under the sole and button-fastened up the sides.

Slow starters, fast finishers

Although today a familiar fastening for boots and shoes, the zip didn't come into general use until the second half of the 20th century.

Stretchy fastenings

The buttons on these Victorian boots are simply decorations. The boots' elastic sides made pulling them on and off far easier and quicker.

Sticky strips

Velcro was introduced as a shoe fastening in the late 20th century. A Swiss engineer called Georges de Mestral got the idea for it in the 1940s, when pulling plant burs from his trousers.

Slip on a sandal

THE SANDAL IS ONE OF THE OLDEST *kinds of shoe, with an open, airy structure that makes it ideal footwear for hot weather. The earliest ancient Egyptians made simple thong-style sandals from papyrus reeds, but in later years they also used palm fronds or leather. Wall paintings show that the nobility had jewels woven into sandals they wore on special occasions.*

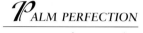

Palm perfection

Woven from palm fronds, this Egyptian sandal was the forerunner of the plastic thong or flip-flop worn worldwide today.

Design developments

The ancient Greeks wore a simple leather sole strapped to the foot, with the ties sometimes continuing a short way up the leg. It was the Romans who reworked the basic design, however, making a more complex sandal from a lattice of woven leather.

In the ancient world, sandals were a sign of wealth and slaves often went barefoot. It was a different story in the chilly climate of northern Europe. During the Middle Ages, sandals were the footwear of monks and priests and were regarded as a sign of their piety and frugal lifestyles.

Air conditioning

The open top and latticework sides of this Roman sandal allowed air to circulate around the foot. Roman sandals were designed to support the foot and could reach well above the ankle.

Eastern elegance

Sandals have been worn in Japan for centuries. The lady on the right's wooden sandals are called getas and, along with the kimono, they are part of Japan's traditional costume.

Shock absorbers

Even on cool days, a long-distance walk can be sweaty work. The latest trekking sandals cushion the sole while letting the rest of the foot breathe.

Style statements

By the 1930s, improvements in shoe technology had made a strappy, high-heeled sandal possible, and this style became a top fashion item. The sandals displayed the neat toe seam of the latest nylon stockings to their best advantage, along with the newly respectable painted toenails.

The hippie movement of the 1960s ushered in a craze for flat leather sandals including Indian sandals which were held on by a loop around the big toe. A decade later, orthopaedic exercise shoes hit the high street, as Birkenstocks and wooden-soled Dr Scholl's sandals became fashionable.

The final decade of the 20th century saw the development of the ultra-comfortable, high-tech trekking sandal (above).

Old favourites

Plastic thong or flip-flop style sandals were given a fashion makeover in 2000–01. Soles were brightly coloured and patterned, while the thong was transparent, beaded or decorated with flowers.

Happy hippies

Cheap leather sandals were an essential part of the colourful, loose-fitting hippie look of the 1960s.

Sporting chances

SPECIAL SHOES FOR SPORT *are a fairly recent development in the history of footwear. They were largely the result of the wider understanding of the value of exercise in building and maintaining health that grew up during the 19th century.*

Playing the field

In Britain, for instance, exercise periods were built into the timetables of all private and publicly funded schools in the 19th century. Heavy boots, often with steel toecaps and metal-studded soles, were worn for football and rugby.

The rubber-soled canvas sports shoe known as the plimsoll was patented in 1876. Relatively cheap to buy, it opened the way for a wider range of sports to be undertaken in school and out. Meanwhile, the popularity of the bicycle led to boots with broad heels for gripping the pedals.

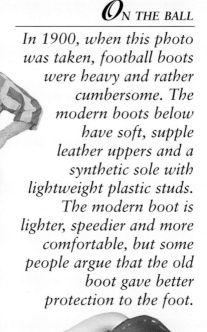

On the Ball

In 1900, when this photo was taken, football boots were heavy and rather cumbersome. The modern boots below have soft, supple leather uppers and a synthetic sole with lightweight plastic studs. The modern boot is lighter, speedier and more comfortable, but some people argue that the old boot gave better protection to the foot.

Get your skates on

Invented in the 18th century, roller skating soon became a fashionable hobby. The skates above date from the 1880s, when they were strapped to ordinary shoes. Contemporary inline skates (right) come attached to specially designed boots which provide strong ankle support. Inline skating didn't take off until the 1980s, although enthusiasts began developing the sport in the early 20th century.

Often two-tone in colour golfing shoes, like all sports shoes, are the subject of on-going research and redesign. Modelled on men's brogues, today they are sturdy lace-ups with studded soles to provide grip.

HOLD TIGHT

To stop feet slipping out of rock crevices, modern climbing boots have very high-grip rubber soles.

Trainers take to the track

The forerunner of the modern trainer was the canvas All Star basketball shoe, first manufactured by the American Converse company in about 1919. A major technological breakthrough came in 1971, when Bill Bowerman of the Nike company invented the high-traction sole by shaping rubber in his wife's waffle iron. This was rapidly followed by the air sole, in which air-filled pockets cushion the impact of the foot as it pounds against the ground.

The fitness boom of the past 30 years has seen an explosion in the design and manufacture of sports shoes, with models specially engineered for the specific demands of individual sports, from running to rock climbing.

WHAT'S IN A NAME?

In the 1980s, a passion for sports shoes went hand-in-hand with the boom in extreme sports such as BMX and skateboarding. The coolest sportsmen and women didn't wear any old trainers – the label was all. Sports shoe manufacturers such as Adidas, Nike, Reebok and Vans went in and out of fashion favour.

Shoes as art

ALTHOUGH THEIR FUNCTION IS TO PROTECT THE FEET, *shoes can also be beautiful, highly decorative, and even – like the 16th-century Venetian chopine –*

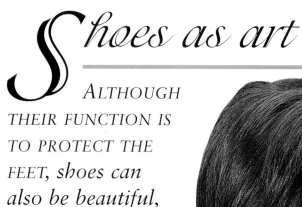

extremely impractical. Advances in shoe manufacturing during the 20th century, and a growing understanding of materials, resulted in innovative one-off designs that are more like works of art than everyday footwear.

MONKEY PUZZLES

In the 1930s, Italian-born fashion designer Elsa Schiaparelli (1890–1973) became famous for her witty and often shocking designs. Made in about 1937, these monkey-fur boots are typical of her surreal sense of humour.

Influenced by artists

Neither art nor design happen in a vacuum, and contemporary clothing and shoe designers are often inspired by the work of painters and sculptors. Some designers start their training in art colleges – Roger Vivier, for instance, originally studied to be a sculptor. In addition to Roger Vivier and Salvatore Ferragamo, leading shoe designers of the 20th century have included Spaniard Manolo Blahnik (*b.*1940), the French designer André Perugia (1893–1977), and British designers Patrick Cox (*b.*1963) and Vivienne Westwood (*b.*1941).

FASCINATED BY FISH

André Perugia created this bizarre fish shoe, complete with tail fins, scales and eyes, in 1931, as a tribute to the still life paintings of the French artist Georges Braque (1882–1963).

SEEING IS BELIEVING?

A painting by the Belgian Surrealist René Magritte (1898–1937), in which clothes and shoes take on the shape of the wearer's body, inspired the extraordinary shoes below. They were created during the 1980s for the French couturier Pierre Cardin (b.1922).

MONDRIAN ON THE MOVE

The abstract, grid-style paintings of Dutch-born artist Piet Mondrian (1872–1944) have influenced everything from fabrics to footwear. These shoes were created in 1950 by the French designer Charles Jourdan (1883–1976).

SCULPTURAL CURVES

Shoemakers have long played with the sculptural possibilities of the platform sole and heel, devising extraordinary variations on their shape.

Men in boots

BOOTS FIRST BECAME A HIGH FASHION ITEM in the 17th century, when the Cavaliers who supported King Charles I of England (1600–49) adopted the riding boot as indoor wear. Cavalier boots, as they became known, were funnel shaped, with a deep cuff at the knee, low heels and spurs.

Birth of the wellington

In the late 18th century, a straight-sided, black riding boot with a contrasting brown top was popularized by the English dandy and fashion leader Beau Brummell (1778–1840). This evolved into the wellington boot. Made of plain black leather in those days, it was named in honour of the Duke of Wellington (1769–1852), who was hailed as a hero after his 1815 victory over the French leader Napoleon (1769–1821) at the Battle of Waterloo.

ROMANTIC ROYALISTS

The Cavaliers were romantic and flamboyant dressers. Their boots were sometimes worn with ornamental spurs (above left and right), or with lace-topped hose, or stockings (above centre).

HERO IN BOOTS

In Britain, the Duke of Wellington (above) was immortalized by the boots named in his honour. Today's wellingtons are made from rubber or plastic, and come in a range of colours.

QUICK MARCH

Armies are famous for marching on their stomachs, but shoes are just as important as food. A pair of sturdy boots has been an important part of the well-equipped soldier's kit since Roman times.

*C*OWBOY GEAR

Cowboy boots have been fashionable since the late 1960s. The pointed toe, curved top and tapered heel are distinctive of the style.

*D*OCTOR KNOWS BEST

Originally designed as work boots, Dr Martens have been worn by groups as diverse as hippies and skinheads. Today they are available in all colours and lengths, from ankle to knee height.

*B*oots hit the high streets

In the 1960s, the prosperity that followed World War II combined with a baby boom to produce large numbers of affluent teenagers. The new shoe styles that catered for this market included the suede desert boot and the Cuban-heeled Beatles boot.

The most enduring boot, however, was the Dr Martens or DM. The original boot was black with yellow stitching, and the first pair rolled off the production line in Britain on 1 April 1960. The DM became standard issue for postmen, police officers and many factory workers, before being taken up by everyone from skinheads to school students.

Women's boots

IN THE PAST, BOOTS WERE WORN only by women who lived in cold climates. The traditional dress of the Inuit peoples of Alaska, northern Canada and Greenland, for instance, has always included animal-skin boots for women as well as for men. In warmer climates, boots were mainly worn by men. The exception was the woman's riding habit, which included leather boots.

Victorian values

The early 19th century saw the tightly laced or buttoned ankle-boot becoming fashionable day wear for women. By the century's end, heeled ankle-boots or the newer calf-length footwear in waterproof leather or cloth were an integral part of the stylish women's wardrobe.

During the first half of the 20th century, it became the rage to display a well-shaped ankle in the new nylon stockings, so boots reverted to being a utilitarian item reserved for bad weather.

Victorian boots

In the 19th century, the calf-length boots worn during the day allowed Victorian women to wear their skirt hemlines fractionally higher, while still modestly covering their ankles.

Women in white

Chic chicks wore white boots in the 1960s, after designer André Courrèges paired them with his miniskirts. The boots came in plastic or leather, and in calf-, knee- and thigh-length.

Runaway success

Skintight leather boots like these reached cult status after they were worn by actress Diana Rigg in the 1960s TV series 'The Avengers'. Such snug-fitting boots would have been impossible without the invention of the zip.

Yeti boots

Shaped like the moon boots of the 1970s, but hairier, the Yeti boot had a high-profile outing when worn by Samantha Mumba at the MOBO awards in 2001.

26

Ringing the changes

The women's fashion boot resurfaced in the 1960s, when French fashion designer André Courrèges (*b.*1923) complemented his sharply angular miniskirts with flat, white boots. When hemlines dropped again in the 1970s, midiskirts were worn over skintight platform boots, but it wasn't until the 1980s and 1990s that boot styles really began to multiply.

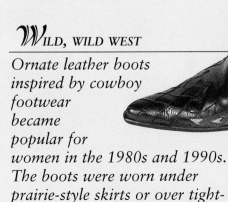

Beauty and the Boot

Thigh-high, stiletto-heeled boots often enjoy a revival when they are worn by a superstar, like Kylie Minogue in 2002.

Wild, wild west

Ornate leather boots inspired by cowboy footwear became popular for women in the 1980s and 1990s. The boots were worn under prairie-style skirts or over tight-fitting denim jeans.

Sturdy fashion

Work boots, such as Dr Martens, for women as well as men, have been in and out of fashion from the sixties until today.

27

Up until the mid-19th century all shoes were made by hand, with shoemakers using virtually the same tools that were around in ancient Egyptian times. The mechanization of shoemaking was made possible by the first practical sewing machine, patented by American inventor Elias Howe (1819–67) in 1846.

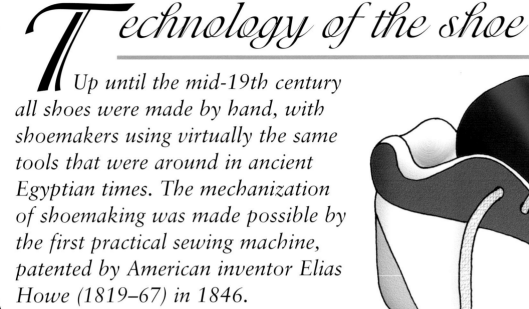

Early automation

Two Americans adapted Howe's invention for use in shoemaking. In 1858 Lyman R. Blake patented a machine for sewing the soles of shoes to uppers. His equipment was improved by Gordon McKay (1821–1903). The next key invention was the shoe-lasting machine, patented in 1883 by American Jan Ernst Matzeliger (1852–89) – the last is a foot-shaped form, over which the upper is shaped and attached to the sole. By the century's end, these and other new machines had led to the mass production of footwear in factories, and the accompanying reductions in cost.

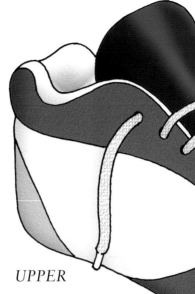

UPPER

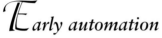

INSERT

MIDSOLE

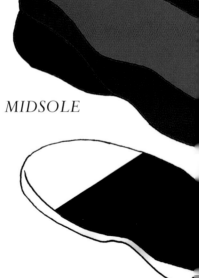

OUTSOLE

Canny computers

Computer-aided design (CAD) programs such as Shoemaster allow contemporary designers to work in 3-D, unlike the 2-D drawings of the past. A CAD design can be rotated to view it from all angles, and colours and other details can be changed in seconds.

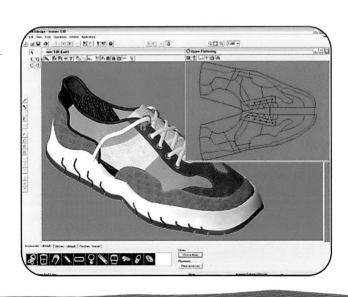

Anatomy of a trainer

The upper, of ever-lighter material, holds the sole on to the foot. The insert is shaped to the foot arch, cushions the foot and helps keep it cool and dry. The crucial midsole gives the most cushioning and is the subject of constant design innovation. The outsole provides grip and, importantly, protects the midsole.

Modern manufacture

These days shoe manufacturing involves dozens of stages, beginning with the design. Once this has been approved, patterns are made for each part in each size of the shoe. The upper parts are cut out and then stitched or glued together. Next the upper is pulled over the last in a lasting machine and stitched or glued to the insole, welt and sole. Finally, a heel is sometimes attached and a removable insert fitted.

Nowadays, computers are involved in many of these stages. Shoes may be designed on a computer, for instance, and manufacturing equipment is often computer-controlled. Some shoes even have computers built into them. Patented in 1999, for instance, the Raven shoe has a battery-powered microchip which responds to the wearer's need for foot cushioning by inflating or deflating a tiny air bladder in the sole!

If the shoe fits

Even the best-designed shoes will harm feet if they don't fit properly. Modern measuring machines use electronic sensors to make an exact map of the foot and judge the correct shoe size.

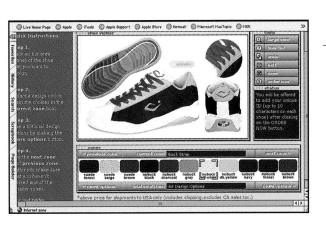

Do it yourself design

Buying footwear via the Internet is old news these days. The new news is that there are websites where you can customize your shoes before they are manufactured, choosing a style and specifying your own materials and colours.

Timeline

Prehistory

In cold regions, the first shoes were animal skins wrapped around the feet or sewn into foot bags.

The ancient world

The ancient Egyptians made papyrus sandals as early as 3700 BCE. By the 1st century CE, the Romans were making shoes with uppers, insoles and tough, hobnailed soles. Their footwear was far more complex than anything else worn at the time, but after the fall of their empire in the 5th century CE, the Romans' shoemaking skills were forgotten.

The Middle Ages

In Europe, in the following centuries, people wore a simple, slipperlike shoe known as the turnshoe after its method of construction. By the 14th century, turnshoes were long and narrow with pointed toes. In the following century, this style gave way to the wide-toed duckbill shoe. By the end of the Middle Ages, the turnshoe was being replaced by a new method of construction, the welted shoe.

16th century

In Venice, women adopted an extreme style called the chopine which had very high platform soles. Elsewhere, heels were attached to the soles of riding boots, to help keep the foot in the stirrup. Court nobles wore high-heeled shoes to exaggerate their height and social status. Shoemakers found heeled shoes more difficult to make. To overcome this, they made shoes with straight sides – there was no distinction between the right and the left foot.

17th century

At the French court, shoes with very high heels were worn by both men and women. Made of wood, the heels were shaped and covered with the same fine cloth as the shoe. Cavalier boots were fashionable footwear for the supporters of King Charles I of England (1600–49). The boots were funnel shaped and knee length, with deep, cuffed tops. During the reign of King Charles II (1630–85), heeled shoes became fashionable again for men, this time decorated with a large, soft bow.

18th century

Stylish men either wore shoes with large buckles, or long, straight, black riding boots. For most of the century, women wore heeled shoes, but when the high-waisted gown came in at the end of the century, heeled shoes were replaced by flat slippers.

19th century

Women's shoes continued to be flat until the second half of the century. Boots started to be reserved for riding and other outdoor pursuits. In the 1830s, elastic-sided boots were introduced and became an immediate success for day wear. The canvas, rubber-soled sports shoe known as the plimsoll was first made in the 1870s. From the middle of the century onwards, shoemaking was revolutionized by the invention of specialist machinery. By the century's end, footwear was again being made in left and right fittings.

20th century & beyond

A wide range of styles were available for men by the early 1900s, and in the 1920s brogues became popular. Women's styles began to vary, as skirt lengths rose and shoes became more visible. The knee-length flapper dress of the 1920s was worn with barred shoes that had decorated heels. The stiletto heel was invented in the mid-1950s and became an enduring style. By the 1960s, stylish young men were wearing pointed-toed shoes such as winkle-pickers. This decade also saw the British launch of the Dr Martens boot. The platform shoe came back into fashion in the 1970s, and in the 1980s advances in synthetic materials and manufacturing led to the creation of the high-tech trainer. By the beginning of the 21st century, footwear fashions were changing with the seasons, with designers borrowing from the past and looking to the future.

Glossary

Brogue

A laced man's shoe with punched decoration on the upper, which became fashionable in the 1920s.

Chopine

An extremely high platform shoe, worn in the 16th century by Venetian ladies.

Cuban heel

A medium-height heel with a slightly tapered back, which first appeared in the 1900s.

Desert boot

A suede ankle-boot with a crepe sole, and short laces, originally developed for soldiers taking part in desert campaigns during World War II.

Last

A foot-shaped form on which the upper is shaped and then attached to the sole.

Louis heel

A medium-height heel, tapered on all sides and flared at the base.

Plimsoll

A sports shoe with a canvas upper and rubber sole, first worn in the 1870s.

Sole

The underside of a shoe, without the heel.

Tread

The part of a shoe sole that touches the ground, often grooved to provide grip.

Turnshoe

A shoe named for its method of construction – the upper and sole were stitched together, then the shoe was turned inside out. The turnshoe was worn in Europe throughout the Middle Ages, until replaced by the welted shoe.

Upper

The parts of a shoe above the sole.

Wellington boot

A waterproof boot, today made from rubber or plastic. Also known as a gumboot.

Welted shoe

A form of shoe construction introduced towards the end of the Middle Ages and still used today. The welt is a strip placed between the insole and sole, and then stitched to them.

Winkle-picker

A shoe with a long, narrow, pointed toe, so-called from the practice of picking winkles (shellfish) from their shells with a long, thin skewer, in order to eat them!

Index